The Creating Formula by Stephen E. Dew.

First Edition

Publisher's Name - HBICambodia.com

PO Box 1736, Phnom Penh, Cambodia. 12000.

Table of Contents

1. To The ESL Student

I have successfully taught academic writing to ESL students for over 3 years now, and I feel well qualified to provide the following reference material as an electronic essay writing handbook on academic writing skills. The great thing about this book is that International ESL students around the world can carry it anywhere they go by using their android, apple, or e-reader devices like Kindle and Nook. What a great resource to have when you need it!

Let's look at what *Practical Academic Essay Writing Skills* will do for you. Clearly, you have a strong desire to increase or improve your knowledge and English academic writing skills or learn how to write a better academic English essay. I am sure finding answers to your questions or achieving your goals are high on your list of expectations.

So what will you get from this book? If you **APPLY** the learning from *Practical Academic Essay Writing Skills* you will:

1) Improve your basic essay writing knowledge and skills.
2) Look much more adept and professional in your essays.

3) Show your classmates how easy essay academic writing really is.

4) Impress your professor at university or your regular English class instructor.

5) Boost your self-confidence in English essay writing.

Moreover, your grades will improve. Let's face it. That's what you want, isn't it? That's why you bought the book. You bought it to provide the answers to your questions. **APPLY** the learning and get the results you want! It's all up to you once you have finished reading this book.

I do wish anyone using this academic essay writing guide the best of luck in improving their English writing skills. However, in saying that, it's not up to luck so much as dedication, hard work, and a personal interest in improving your English academic writing skills. **APPLY** your newly learned knowledge with practical essay writing skills, and you can write you way to a BA.

2. Introduction

Practical Academic Essay Writing Skills: An International ESL Students Essay Writing Handbook is the second book in my series on "Academic Writing Skills".

The book was designed as a supplementary handbook for non-English speaking International ESL Students but by no means only for ESL students wanting to learn English Academic Writing. It can also be used by anyone wishing to understand more about academic essay writing.

Although *Practical Academic Essay Writing Skills* is the second book in the series, it must be said that you do not have to read the first book, *Learn English Paragraph Skills*, however, in saying that, I do recommend that you read it, as it does provide the basis for a well-developed, organized, and written paragraph, especially, the section on the academic English writing process. The paragraph writing skills discussed in *Learn English Paragraph Skills (Paragraph Essentials)* are required when trying to create much larger content like essays for your readers.

As I stated in my address to the purchaser, it is

extremely important you APPLY the leanings from this book if you want to improve your English essay writing skills.

Note: Although I have included some examples for clarity, I have intentionally left out practice exercises, as that is not the intention of this guide. International ESL students get plenty of practice in their regular classes, so this was written to supplement those classes with easy to read reference material. If you are looking for some practice exercises, try *"English Writing Exercises for International Students: An ESL Grammar Workbook for ESL Essay Writing."* This is an Interactive Workbook written to support all my books in the series *"Academic Writing Skills.*

Let's get started shall we!

3. Essay Types

There are many different types of essays you will be expected to write. The most common types of essay you will be asked to write when studying academically will probably be:

> ➢ Comparison and Contrast Essays
> ➢ Definition Essays
> ➢ Opinion Essays
> ➢ Logical Division Essays
> ➢ Narrative Stories
> ➢ Process Essays (how to do something)

The types of essays listed above are not the topic of this book; however, I will touch on them in the next few pages. Also, I use them to demonstrate the academic essay writing process.

I will cover these specific topics in more detail in future book releases. So for now, let's focus on the reasons you purchased this book, *Practical Academic Essay Writing Skills*, and hopefully provide the information you are looking for to improve your English academic writing skills.

a) Comparison and Contrast

A comparison describes two or more things that are similar, whereas, a contrast describes differences. These types of essays usually tell readers about similarities or differences between two things. Most of these kinds of essays are generally contrast, but of course, you can write about both similarities and differences in the same essay.

Comparison and contrast essays are used quite widely for academic studies. This kind of essay usually results in some kind of recommendation based on your research and analysis. Comparison and Contrast essays demonstrate your analytical and decision making process based on data like examples, facts, or statistics.

b) Definition Essays

Definition essays are used to define or explain something like a word or an idea, or you may need to explain an abstract concept. These kinds of essays are also used widely in academic studies. They show your ability to define, explain, and understand the meaning of a concept or idea.

c) Opinion Essays

Opinion essays are important in academic studies too. Students, college graduates, and even people working for corporate companies are asked every day to provide an opinion formally and to support their opinion. This style of writing shows the reader what you think and why. Reasons and examples are extremely important in these kinds of essays.

d) Logical Division

One other common kind of essay you may be asked to write is a pattern of organization in which you divide your topic into points that are discussed separately. We call this kind of essay logical division of ideas. In these essays, you discuss points one by one in some kind of logical order such as most important to least important using words like:

- ➤ reasons
- ➤ kinds
- ➤ types
- ➤ advantages or disadvantages
- ➤ qualities
- ➤ characteristics.

➢   ways

These kinds of essays are general essays because each paragraph usually discusses one main idea of the overall essay topic. For example, look at these topics and think of some main points that would be discussed in a paragraph of an essay.

- *Type of mobile phones.*
- *Kinds of students.*
- *Reason to own an iPad*
- *Advantages / disadvantages of learning a new language.*
- *Qualities of a good friend.*
- *Characteristics of a good teacher.*

You can easily see that the points discussed are usually one by one or point by point.

4. Essay Organization

Is essay organization more any difficult than paragraph organization? Well not really. It's a little more time consuming, however, the time spent reflects the effort, and the effort reflects on the final product.

So, what's the difference between an essay and a paragraph? A paragraph is a group of sentences discussing similar or related ideas of a topic. In academic writing there are three parts to any paragraph. There is the topic sentence, the body, and the concluding sentence. You can read more about these concepts in my first book, *Learn English Paragraph Skills*.

An essay is a connected group of paragraphs. An essay is longer. One important thing to note about essays is not only are they longer, but you must also plan an essay with much more care. The more planning with an essay; the better the result; the better the result; the better your grade, and let's face it. That's what you're after, isn't it? A better grade!

Essays, the same as paragraphs, must have unity and coherence. Without following these two rules, your essay will not be logical and well presented. It may actually be difficult to read, and your message may not be understood by your reader or professor.

An essay must also contain transition signals, varied sentence openings, and maintain parallel structure the same as paragraphs.

a) Unity

Unity is a term used to describe in my words, "*one idea - one paragraph*". That means that all of your supporting sentences in a paragraph discuss only ideas directly related to the main idea of the paragraph. Remember, when writing English academically, it is not acceptable to deviate from the main topic of a paragraph.

b) Coherence

Paragraphs should follow the rule of coherence. A coherent paragraph runs like water, smoothly, from start to finish. Any reader can easily follow the ideas being presented in a paragraph because they are logically connected, and each sentence leads naturally to the next.

To achieve coherence in your essay follow these

guidelines:

- Use consistent nouns and pronouns in your paragraphs. Don't mix them!
- Use transition signals to show the relationship between sentence details within your paragraphs.
- Maintain logical order within your essay by using transition signals that show the relationship between your paragraphs.
- Vary your sentence openings.
- Use parallel structure.

c) Transition Signals

Transition signals play a very important role in essays. Not only do they connect ideas within paragraphs, they also connect the related paragraphs. They are the traffic lights of English writing. They tell reader what is going to happen and the relationships between sentences and paragraphs.

This is a concept that must be understood, for an essay must clearly show your ideas or opinions logically, so the reader can understand and follow you.

d) Varying Sentence Openings

You might be asking, "Why would I vary my sentence openings in paragraphs?" Well the simple answer is it makes your essay more interesting, and shows that you understand what you are doing. Simply put, it helps you look more professional when writing academic English.

When writing sentences, you vary the type of sentence, and the start of a sentence. For example, start a sentence with a prepositional phrase (don't forget to add a comma after the prepositional phrase). Use appositives to give more meaning and definition to nouns, or alternatively, you can start with a dependent clause before the independent clause (again, don't forget to add a comma after the dependent clause).

Furthermore, one other important point to remember is the type of transition signal used between paragraphs of an essay can also be varied to make things flow smoothly.

If you adopt these concepts, you will look much more adept and professional, and I know that this is one of your goals for learning academic essay writing. So, a good tip when writing academically is to vary your sentence openings.

e) Parallel Structure

Finally, here is a note on parallel structure. When you write a sentence with a series of words or clauses, make sure that they start and end using the same form. If you don't, you will destroy the coherence you've tried to establish. More importantly, Robert M Knight said in an article I read, *"If you use parallel structures your readers will have a more enjoyable time absorbing and understanding your facts, ideas, and concepts."* (Robert M. Knight, *A Journalistic Approach to Good Writing*. Wiley, 2003).

Once again, I know one of your goals is for your readers to enjoy, absorb, and understand what you have written. Write for your reader, not yourself.

f) Review Check

Are you still with me? If not, go back and re-read what I said about essay organization. It is important you understand essay organization, and the concepts I have spoken about.

You can also ask me any questions about these concepts by visiting my website contact page mentioned in the Author profile at the end of this book.

5. Essay Structure

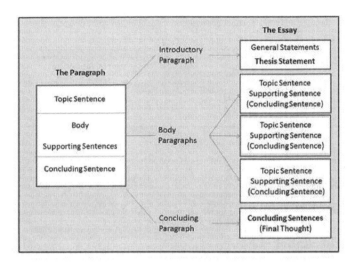

Now that you have understood essay organization, let's look at essay structure. An essay will have a minimum of three paragraphs, and as with a paragraph, there are three parts to an essay:

➢ The Introductory Paragraph
➢ The Body Paragraphs
➢ The Concluding Paragraph

a) The Introductory Paragraph

An introduction should attract the reader's interest,

and it should tell the reader what they are going to read and the kind of essay. It is one of the most important paragraphs in your essay. It contains a few general statements, and the last sentence in the introduction is usually the thesis statement but not always.

Writing an introductory paragraph is similar to meeting somebody for the first time. It's like saying hello to someone to make sure you leave a good impression with the person you meet. Similarly, an essay introduction must leave a good impression and attract the reader's interest.

The introductory paragraph should be short (but at least 50 words), and it has three functions:

- It briefly introduces the topic.
- It clearly states your position on the topic.
- It provides at least three main ideas.

There are few ways to write an introduction. These are the most common types of introduction:

- General statement introduction.
- Question introduction.
- Quotation introduction.

We will only look the general statement introduction. This type of introduction is the most commonly used way to start an essay when learning English essay writing.

i.   General Statement Introduction

A general statement introduction has a few general statements providing the reader with the background of the topic. The first general statement introduces the topic of the essay. The following general statements should lead the reader gradually to the thesis statement. That means each general statement becomes more specific and more focused on the topic. The last sentence in a general statement introduction is the thesis statement.

Remember to state your specific topic and controlling idea in the thesis statement.

ii.   What is a Thesis Statement and what does it do?

The thesis statement is what defines the topic and controlling idea of your essay. In a thesis statement you name the topic and state the controlling idea. The controlling idea specifies the scope of the essay. It tells the reader what you are writing about the topic. It restricts your essay to specific ideas on the topic.

The thesis statement has three purposes:

- It states the specific topic of the essay.
- It can list the main ideas of your topic.
- It can tell the reader the pattern of organization used.

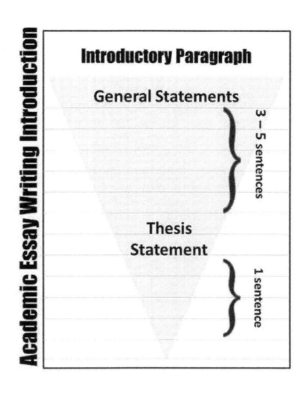

b) The Body Paragraphs

The essay body consists of one or more connected paragraphs which discuss the main ideas of the topic in more detail. They also include references to your examples being fact, real life examples, or reported detail from your research.

In the previous paragraph, I said, "... *connected paragraphs...*" This is where transition between paragraphs is essential to make sure the essay flows smoothly.

i.   Transitions Between Paragraphs

Transitions between paragraphs in your essay play a very important role. As I stated earlier, sentence transition signals connect the ideas within a paragraph. Paragraph transition signals tell your reader if the topic of the next paragraph continues with same line of thinking as the previous paragraph, or if the next paragraph changes to an opposite line of thinking.

For Transition Signals you will notice not only sentence connectors but a few prepositions. The advantage of using prepositions as paragraph transition signals is you can repeat the topic of the previous paragraph, whilst naming the topic of the next paragraph. By using this method of paragraph transition, you can link your body paragraphs as a logical, connected, and coherent essay.

For example: In addition to creating connected sentences, transition signals connect paragraphs.

ii. Supporting Evidence For the Body of Your Essay

A few ways to develop supporting detail for your essay is to use examples, quotations, or facts like statistics. These are very powerful ways to show your reader convincingly how you support your topic, opinion, or research.

Giving examples can be done by using words like:

- for example,
- for instance,
- such as
- like

When using statistics, you may quote information from magazines, books, newspapers, interviews, or the internet. If using quotes, make sure you follow the rules for reported speech (see appendix).

iii.   A Note on Plagiarism

If you look up the word plagiarism on the internet or in a dictionary, it gives a very descriptive definition. All of this simply put means, if you plagiarize, you steal other people's words, images, or ideas. When writing academically, it is OK to use other people's work, but you must give credit to the source of the information. This is called citation (see appendix).

c) The Concluding Paragraph

In academic essay writing, the essay conclusion is the last paragraph, and it has three functions.

- It tells the reader the essay is finished.
- It helps the reader to remember your main ideas.
- It leaves the reader with your final thought about the topic.

Concluding paragraphs in essays are similar to paragraph conclusions. They summarize or restate the main ideas of the essay.

One difference is that you can use more than one sentence to write your conclusion in an essay. Also, sometimes writers leave a final thought to prompt the reader or give the reader something to think about when they have finished reading. This helps the reader to remember what you have written, and it gets them to think more deeply about your ideas on the topic.

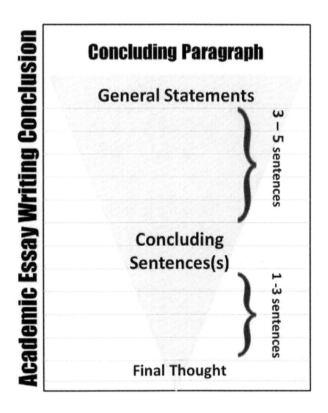

d) Review Check

OK for now?

Essay structure is certainly not difficult, but it is something that you must adhere to, so as to have a good consistent and convincing essay.

Are you still with me?

If not, go back and re-read what I said about essay structure. It is important you understand essay structure, and the concepts I have spoken about.

You can also ask me any questions about these concepts by visiting my website contact page mentioned in the Author profile at the end of this book, or possibly read my first book "*Learn English Paragraph Writing Skills*".

Now let's look at an outline for an essay.

6. Essay Outline

Outlining is a process that helps organize your ideas before you begin to write. It is like building a house. You must have a plan or else the house may end up with walls too high, too short, too long, or perhaps you miss a door! Having a plan not only helps you organize your ideas, it also makes sure you don't forget to add your most important ideas.

When creating an outline for an essay, planning is much more important because you have a lot of ideas and details to organize and support.

As you create the outline, you indent as you move from Roman numerals to capital letters to numbers to small letters. I have attached an image of what a detailed outline looks like.

Look at the numbering system used below:

- The introduction, body, and concluding paragraph use Roman numerals (I, II, and III).
- The topic sentence of each paragraph uses capital letter (A, B, and so on).
- Each main supporting idea uses numbers (1, 2, and so

on).

- Each supporting point uses small letters (a, b, and so on).

Please note: you should also include your examples in your outline, so you don't forget to add them to your essay.

If this process is done correctly, your essay writing process steps are much more simplified, and your essay will be assured of maintaining coherence because you have added your transitions as well into the outline.

Detailed Essay Outline

I.   Thesis Statement

II. Body

    A. Topic Sentence
       1. Main Supporting Idea
          a. Supporting detail
          b. Supporting detail
          c. Supporting detail
       2. Main Supporting Idea
          a. Supporting detail
          b. Supporting detail
       3. Main Supporting Idea
          a. Supporting detail
          b. Supporting detail
          (Concluding Sentence)

    B. Topic Sentence
       1. Main Supporting Idea
          a. Supporting detail
          b. Supporting detail
       2. Main Supporting Idea
          a. Supporting detail
          b. Supporting detail
          c. Supporting detail
       3. Main Supporting Idea
          a. Supporting detail
          b. Supporting detail
          (Concluding Sentence)

    C. Topic Sentence
       1. Main Supporting Idea
          a. Supporting detail
          b. Supporting detail
       2. Main Supporting Idea
          a. Supporting detail
          b. Supporting detail
       3. Main Supporting Idea
          a. Supporting detail
          b. Supporting detail
          c. Supporting detail
          (Concluding Sentence)

III. Concluding Sentences (and final thought)

Do not forget to include examples and transition signals

7. Review to Date

So now you have looked at:

- Essay Types
- Essay Organization
- Essay Structure
- Essay Outlines

It is important you understand all these steps. If you do not understand, go back then read them again. Do not forget, you can also ask me some questions on my website contact page. Also, you should take time to review the appendices as well.

Now we are now going to discuss the essay writing process. This process is tried and true. That means you can use it for every essay you write to maintain good consistent results. You **MUST** follow this process. If you do not follow this process for your essay writing, your essays will be uninteresting, confusing, and seemingly immature. Furthermore, you will not receive good grades from professors or lecturers.

Why? I heard you ask!

The problem I find is ESL students want the result without effort. Well, it can't be done, and I'll stick to using the academic writing process for great results. After years of writing, I still use this basic process for writing my essays, articles, and now books.

You should practice this until it becomes second nature. When you become proficient in the academic essay writing process, you will become a proficient and skilled writer.

So let's move on to the essay writing Process, shall we!

8. The English Essay Writing Process

The 5 Step Essay Writing Process

In this section I am going to describe the essay writing process you should use. It is extremely important you understand each step. By following each step, you will be assured of a much better essay, and hence a much better result.

It is time to put your knowledge into action!

a) Pre Write

Pre write is the first step you use in the academic essay writing process. Pre writing helps you to get ideas about a topic.

In this step, you write down your ideas in any way or form that helps you remember your ideas. Most ELS students prefer to do a brainstorm or cluster, however, the other techniques such as listing, free writing, and note taking discussed in my first book, *Learn English Paragraph Writing Skills*, are just as friendly to use.

Use a technique that you like and are comfortable with. I particularly like clustering because it helps me with some pre organizing while I'm thinking of new ideas. I'm sure if you use clustering, you too will like the way it helps you pre organize your ideas as well.

b) Organize

Most students tend to understand outlining, but they fail to recognize that doing an outline is actually a part of the organize step.

When you organize your pre-writing you follow these two sub steps.

1. First, you look at your list and group your ideas logically. Circle the ideas you want to use. Delete the ideas you believe are unnecessary or are duplicated

points. Sometimes, your ideas may be better organized into a table with category headings, so that you can use the categories for your main ideas.

2. Once this part is completed, you do an outline. An outline helps you organize or arrange your ideas in a logical order. In my example of building a house, first, you lay the foundations. Then you build the walls. Finally you add the roof. Your outline is the foundation of your essay. Outlines can be simple or detailed. When writing essays, I suggest you use a detailed outline.

Referring to the figure in section 6 "Essay Outline", the number of main supporting points can be more or less, and the amount of supporting detail can be more or less. It all depends on you, and how much you need to write. You may have no supporting detail for a particular main idea, or you may have five or six supporting sentences. The amount of detail is up to you!

When writing your outline, include you paragraph transition signals and your supporting evidence such as your examples, quotes, facts, or statistics you have found. Including this detail at this stage of the essay writing process will help when it comes to putting pen to paper in the next step.

c) First Draft

As I said previously, step 3 is where you put pen to paper. Here you follow your outline to write your first draft. Write it as quickly as possible, and don't worry about too many mistakes. It's OK to make some mistakes at this stage because after all, it is only a draft. You will fix any errors you make in the next step. At this stage of writing, it is perfectly acceptable to add any new ideas you think of.

To help you understand a little more, when writing larger essays or other types of academic writing, chunk you time. What do I mean? I mean write in blocks of time, so you do not get confused or burnt out. In brief, plan you writing time for larger academic essay writing assignments.

To start, you begin by writing general statements which lead to your thesis statement. Then start writing your paragraphs making sure you use transition signals within the paragraph and between paragraphs. Pay attention to the rules of unity, coherence, and parallelism. Add varying sentence openings outlined in the section Varying Sentence Openings. Then finally, finish off by using general statements in your concluding paragraph, and write your concluding sentence(s). Don't forget to add a final thought if you want to. A final thought is usually some kind of opinion, recommendation, or judgment.

When writing some kinds of paragraphs, you must provide supporting evidence to prove your point. For example, in opinion essays, you must be able to convince the reader that your opinion is the right one. Your essay may help them to change their mind. Another example is in definition paragraphs where you may be required to explain something, so don't forget to add your examples from your outline into your essay and ensure you cite your references as well.

Also note when you have finished your first draft, you may need to write a second draft if you want a great essay. I sometimes do this if I want the perfect essay.

You too could try this to see if your results improve.

d) Edit and Review

In this section, I am not going to repeat what I said in my first book, however, I have provided a reference to the information in the appendix at the back of this book for a quick look at the details covered in my first book, *Learn English Paragraph Writing Skills.*

We normally do two kinds of reviews for our academic essay writing.

1) Peer Review
2) Self-Edit

e) Start Writing

Once you have your feedback from your peer review and completed your self-edit, you should write your final polished version. Don't forget to add your reference list at the end of your essay or article if you have cited information.

Again, you may need to rewrite your essay for that perfect grade! Once done, you're finished.

Now congratulate yourself!

For more details on The English Essay Writing Process visit my author page at Amazon.com and discover "*The 5 Step Essay Writing Process*".

9. Summary and Conclusion

You are now fully equipped to write an excellent essay, assignment, article, or thesis for that matter for your university course. By following the five step academic writing process, you can write your way to a BA, so don't forget that!

I remember in my first book, *Learn English Paragraph Writing Skills - Paragraph Essentials*, I said, "Academic writing was simple." Even though I said simple, I really meant that it was not difficult if you follow the academic essay writing process.

It also means you must understand the theory as well. Moreover, you must spend more time, more planning, and more effort, but consider the rewards of learning about a practical academic essay writing process.

The specific details we have covered in this eBook were:

- Essay Types
- Essay Organization
- Essay Structure
- Essay Outline

- Essay Writing Process

You should put an electronic copy of this book on your personal electronic devices. If you do, you can carry the information with you, and you will be able to use it as a quick essay writing reference whenever you need it. You can also use it to supplement your regular English writing tutorials in class. If you combine your learned theory with the practical academic essay writing process, you will become a proficient academic writer in no time.

I also said rewards, because in other words, as an effective and efficient writer, the sky is the limit.

In conclusion, at the start of this book, we looked at your reasons for buying *"Practical Academic Essay Writing Skills"*.

Let's do a recap of those reasons:

1. Improve your basic essay writing knowledge and skills.

2. Look much more adept and professional in your essays.

3. Show your classmates how easy essay academic writing really is.

4. Impress your professor at university or your regular

English class Instructor.

5.   Boost your self-confidence in English essay writing.

6.   Improve your grades.

You can easily see *"Practical Academic Essay Writing Skills - An International ESL Student Essay Guide"* will help you achieve your goals, but only if you practice essay writing and use the essay writing process until it becomes a part of your academic writing skill set. **APPLY, and I mean APPLY,** your newly learned practical essay writing skills, and you can write you way to a BA.

I sincerely wish you good luck in your academic studies, and truly hope you found this eBook valuable now, and into the future as good reference material for your academic writing skills.

10. Appendix

a) Using Examples

Use of examples and quotes is expected by readers and professors alike. It helps prove your point and creates more authority in your writing.

You can use examples such as:

- reported speech (citation).
- statistical facts.
- real life examples.
- a combination of all of these.

b) Citation

The information in this section was taken from "*Academic writing: Citing sources - Citing APA style.*" This is an abridged version which is probably all you need for now.

There are two ways in which you can refer to, or cite, another person's work:

1. by using direct quotation.
2. by using reporting.

i. Direct Quotation

Examples using quotes can be expressed with words like:

- "He reported,"
- "In his book he stated,"
- "He said,"
- "For example,"
- "such as" or "like".

These are only a few. Use them to show the reader how you are supporting your ideas.

Occasionally you may want to quote another author's words exactly: For example, Hillocks (1982) similarly reviews dozens of research findings. He writes, "The available research suggests that teaching by written comment on compositions is generally ineffective" (p. 267).

Use references at the end of an Essay. For example, Hillocks, G. (1982). The interaction of instruction, teacher comment, and revision in teaching the composing process. Research in the Teaching of English, 16, 261-278.

ii. Reporting

This simply means reporting the other writer's ideas into your own words. You can either paraphrase if you want to keep the length the same or summarize if you want to make the text shorter. There are two main ways (Swales, 1990, p. 148) of showing that you have used another writer's ideas:

Integral

- According to Peters (1983) evidence from first language acquisition indicates that lexical phrases are learned first as unanalyzed lexical chunks.

- Evidence from first language acquisition indicating that lexical phrases are learned first as unanalyzed lexical chunks was given by Peters (1983).

Non-integral

- Evidence from first language acquisition (Peters, 1983) indicates that lexical phrases are learned first as unanalyzed lexical chunks.

- Lexical phrases are learned first as unanalyzed

lexical chunks (Peters, 1983).

If you want to refer to a particular part of the source:

- According to Peters (1983, p. 56) evidence from first language acquisition indicates that lexical phrases are learned first as unanalyzed lexical chunks.

References at the end of an Essay:

- Peters, A (1983). The units of language acquisition. Cambridge: Cambridge University Press.

To see the full article visit Citing Sources website: http://www.uefap.com/writing/writfram.htm

c) Peer Review

A peer review means the peer reviewer should read your paragraph, ask questions about your paragraph, and make some comments on what they think is good or what they think should be changed to make you paragraph more clear.

They do not check for grammar, punctuation, or spelling. The peer reviewer should check for things like:

- Is the topic clear?
- Was the paragraph interesting?
- Did the reviewer learn anything?
- Did they understand everything?
- Do they need more information?
- Should something be included in the paragraph?
- Should something be removed from the paragraph?
- Is the paragraph on topic?
- Is the paragraph coherent?
- Does the conclusion summarize or restate the topic sentence in different words?

d) Self-Edit

A self-edit means you check your draft for any errors. It's like polishing your car. You make sure your paragraph is spic and span for others to read. When you do your self-check you should check for things like:

1.   Is the title appropriate and does it follow the title rules? Note the rules are simple. Capitalize the first and last word in a title, and all the major words. Don't capitalize small words like articles and small prepositions.

2.   Is my paragraph format correct?

3.   Paragraph Organization and Structure

- Does my paragraph address the topic?
- Does my paragraph have a good topic sentence and concluding sentence?
- Do my transition signals connect my ideas correctly?
- If writing an essay, do my transition signals connect my paragraphs?
- Do my examples to support my ideas?
- Does my paragraph follow the rules of unity and coherence?

4.   Grammar and Sentence Structure

- Do I have any sentence errors?
- Have I used a combination of sentence types like simple sentence?
- Compound sentences and complex sentences?
- Have I varied sentence openings by using some prepositional phrases or dependent clauses?

5.   Punctuation and Capitalization

- Have I used a period, question mark, or exclamation mark at the end of each sentence?
- Have used commas according to the commas rules and sentence structure?
- Have I used capitals correctly?
- Is my spelling correct?

e) Commonly used Transition Signals

Usage	Sentence Connectors	Coordinating Conjunctions	Subordinating Conjunctions	Other
To add another or similar idea	Furthermore,	and		
	Also,	both ... and ...		
	In addition,	not only ... but also ...		
	Finally,			
	Moreover,			
	Similarly,			
	Besides,			
To add an opposite idea or contrast	On the other hand,	but	although	different from
	However,	Yet	even though	differently
			though	unlike
			while	differ from
			whereas	differ in

11. References:

- Dew, Stephen E. (2013). *Learn English Paragraph Writing Skills.* Amazon: hbicambodia.com.

- Dew, Stephen E. (2013). *The 5 Step Essay Writing Process.* Amazon: hbicambodia.com.

- Knight, Robert M. (2003). *A Journalistic Approach to Good Writing.* Wiley, 2003.

- Gillett, Andy (2013). *Using English for Academic Purposes. Academic Writing*: Citing Sources, viewed October 16 2004, viewed July 2013, http://www.uefap.com/writing/writfram.htm

12. About the Author: Stephen E. Dew

The author, Stephen E. Dew, is a veteran of 33 years in the Telecommunication Industry from Australia. He obtained an Associate Diploma in Engineering in 1997 and achieved several units towards a Graduate Certificate in Management by 2004. Having relocated to Perth, after 5 Years in Melbourne writing strategic papers for his business unit, he settled in Bedford and began writing as hobby.

In 2008, he left the Telecommunications sector and traveled SE Asia, where he finally settled in Cambodia. In 2010, he obtained his TESOL qualifications and a Graduate Diploma in Enterprise Applied Management in 2011. He now teaches English Academic Writing to Khmer ESL students at a well renowned University in Phnom Penh. Stephen is married and enjoys time with his family, teaching, and writing, which are three of his passions. For more information about the author visit Amazon Author Central.

Please note if you enjoyed or learned something from this book, I would appreciate if you could leave a review on Amazon. To leave a review for "*Practical Academic Essay Writing Skills*", go to Amazon and search for "Practical Academic Essay Writing Skills."

If you wish to follow Academic Writing Skills, or be informed of future book releases and updates, then sign up for our reader's newsletter at:

http://stephenedew.hbicambodia.com/.

You can also follow us on Facebook and / or Twitter.

Discover the series "Academic Writing Skills"

If you are seeking more information about paragraph writing techniques then take a look at book I in the series, Academic Writing Skills, "*Learn English Paragraph Writing Skills: ESL Paragraph Essentials for International Students*".

If you are seeking more information about the English essay writing process then take a look at book III in the series, Academic Writing Skills, "*The 5 Step Essay Writing Process: English Essay Writing Skills for ESL Students*".

If you are looking for some practice exercises, try *"English Writing Exercises for International Students: An ESL Grammar Workbook for ESL Essay Writing."* This is an Interactive Workbook written to support all my books in the series Academic Writing Skills.

Stephen E. Dew

TESOL Instructor and Author

of the series Academic Writing Skills

This page has been left blank

intentionally!

Made in the USA
San Bernardino, CA
29 June 2017